This book is dedicated to my niece and nephew, Aaliyah and Rayan. They brought color and excitement into our world. May the children in your life bring color into yours as well.

This book belongs to

____

Aa

Airplane

Bb

Boat

Cc

Cupcake

Dd

Dragon

Ee

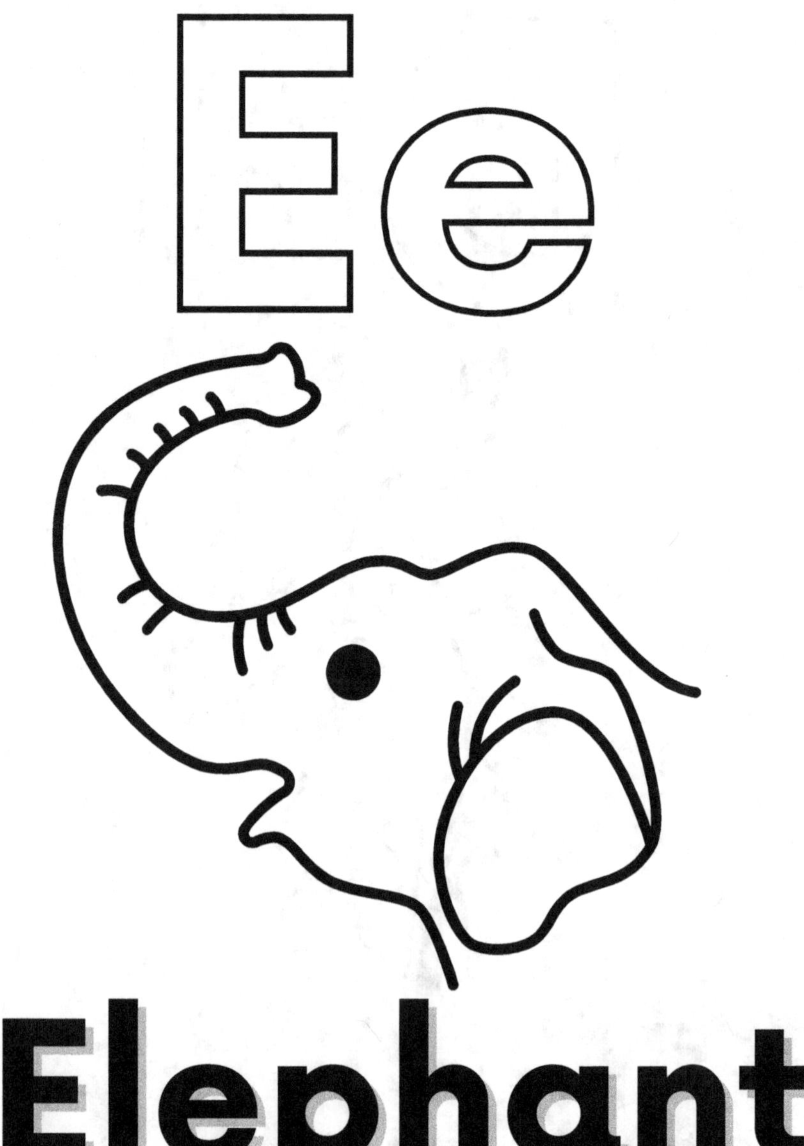

Elephant

Ff

Fire

Gg

Guitar

Hh

Horse

Ii

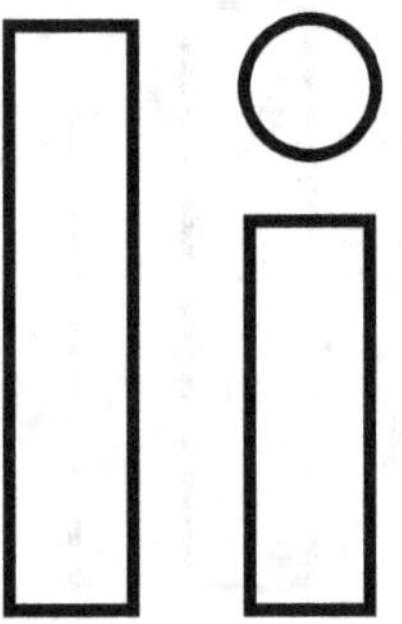

Igloo

Jj

Jacket

Kk

Kite

Ll

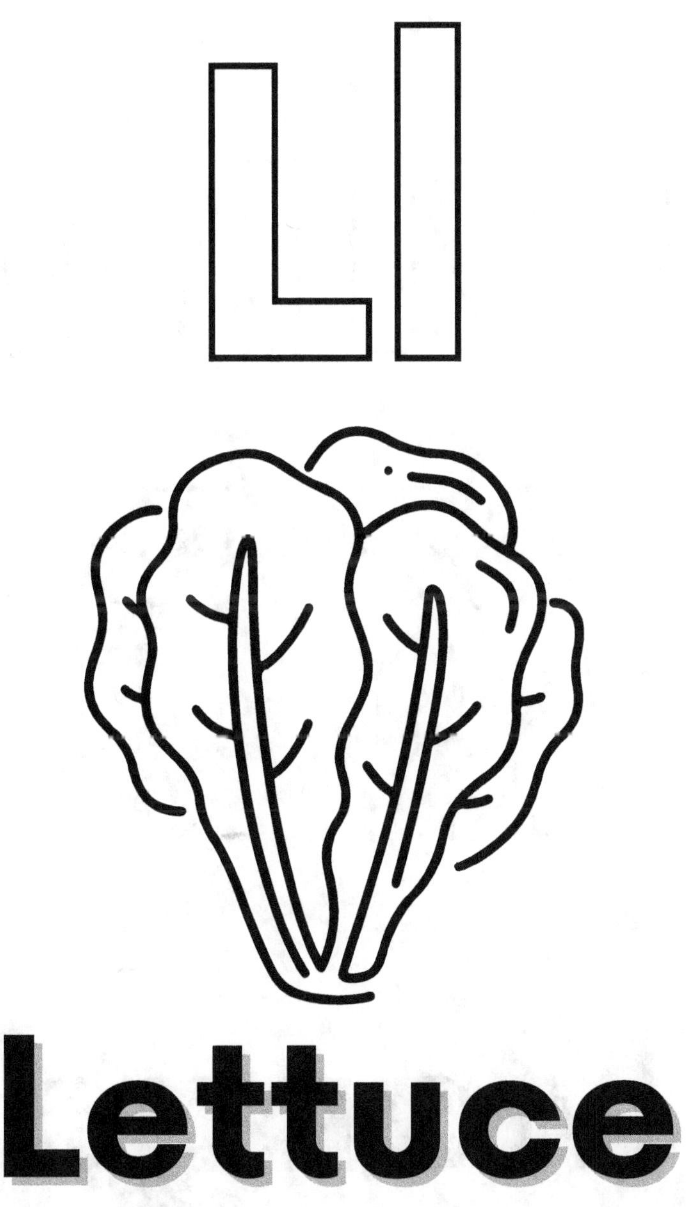

Lettuce

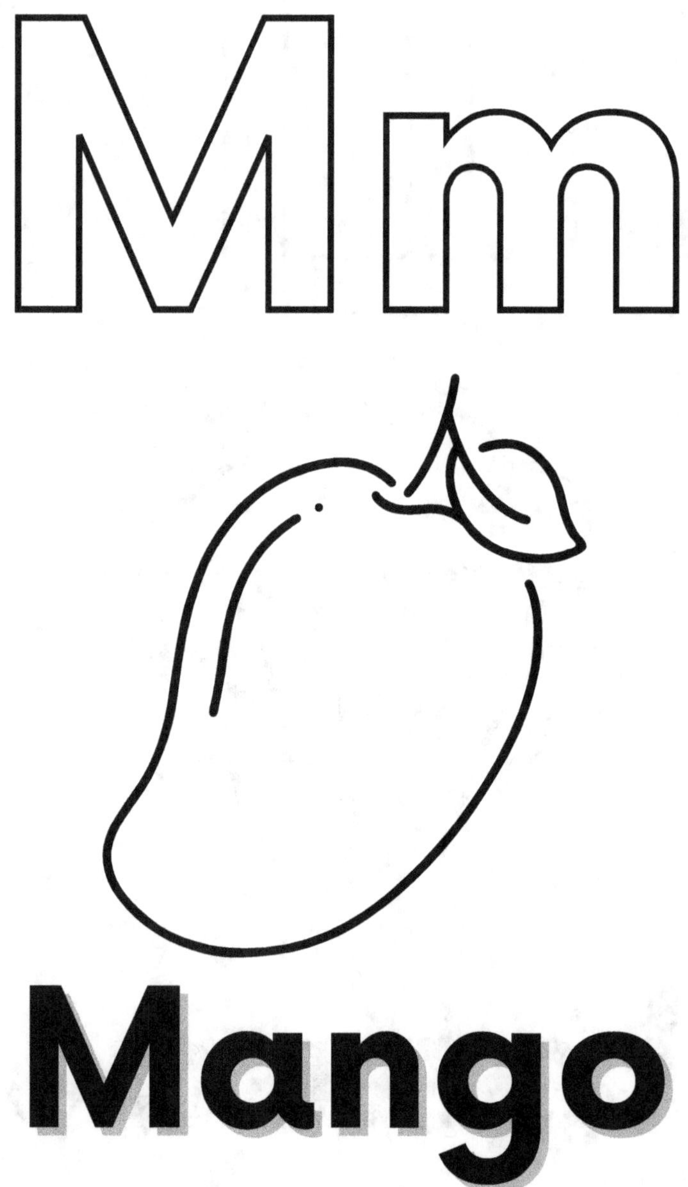

Mm

Mango

Nn

Nurse

Owl

Pp

Pizza

Qq

Queen

R r

Rat

Ss

Spoon

Tt

Tree

U u

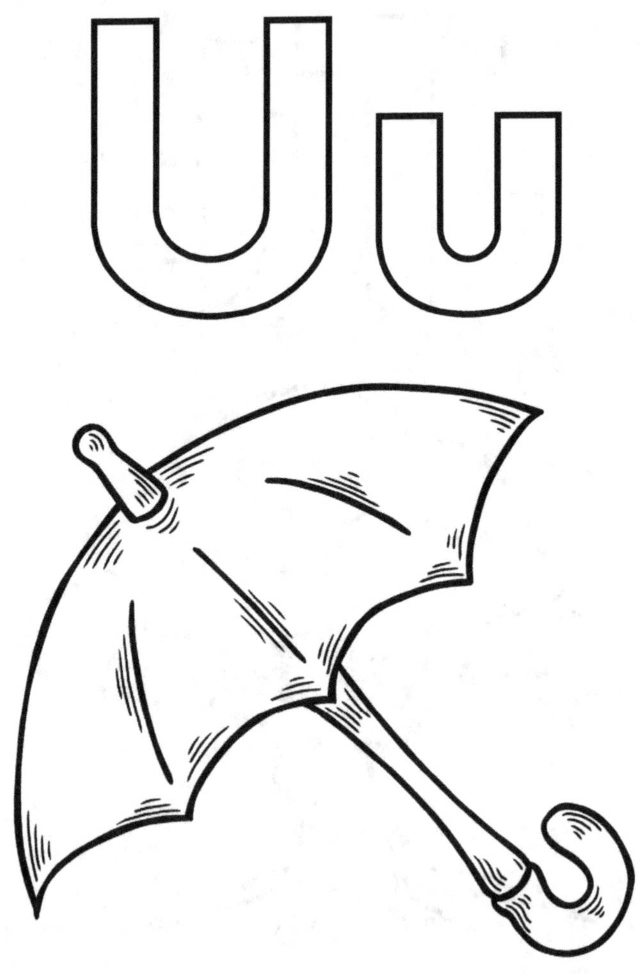

Umbrella

Vv

Vest

Ww

Watch

Xx

X-Ray

Yy

Yoyo

Zz

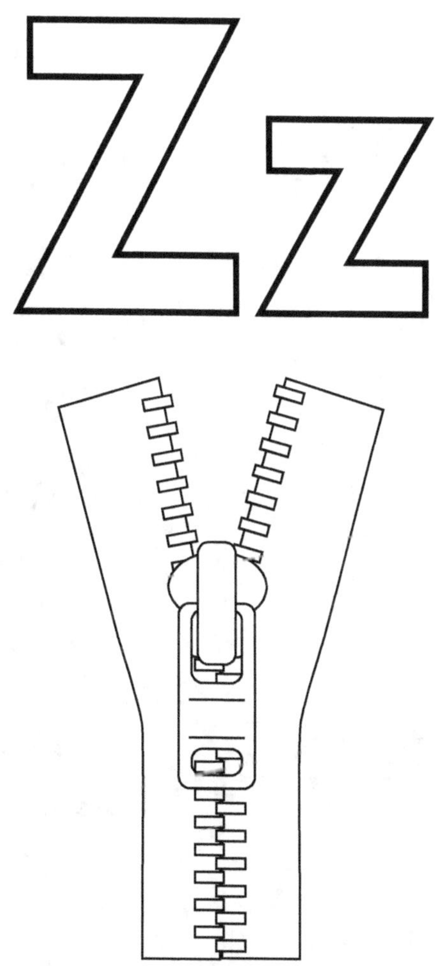

Zipper

Match The Worlds to The Image

Zipper

Rat

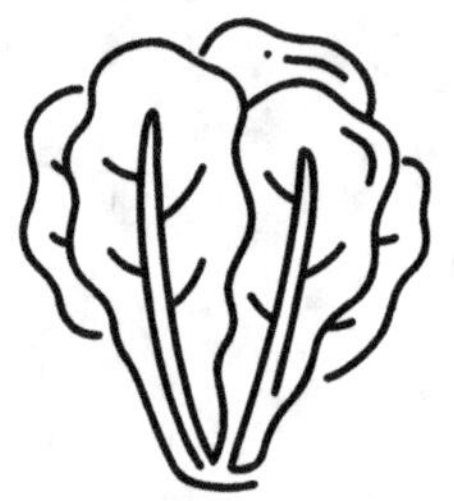

Lettuce

Tree

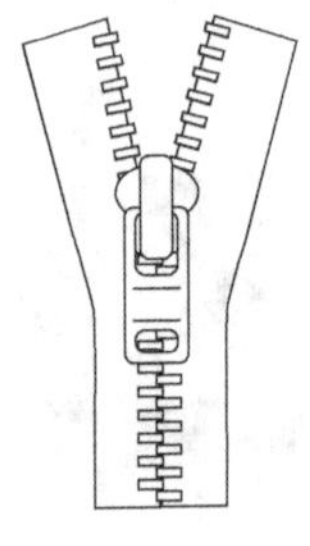

Dragon 

Queen 

X-Ray 

Igloo 

Kite

Watch

Pizza

Yoyo

Horse

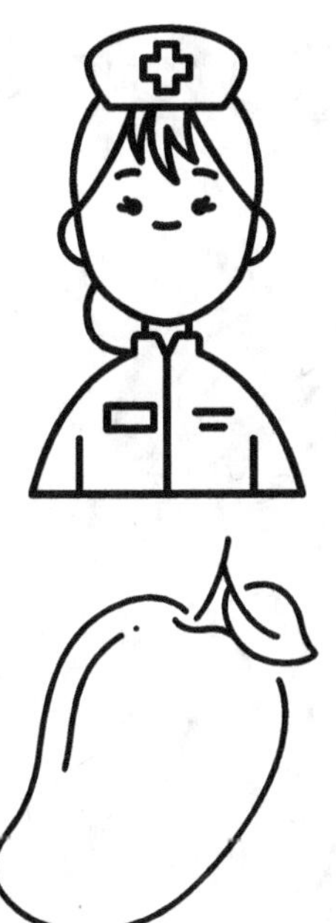

Owl

Mango

Nurse

Color The Animals

Color The Foods

DRAW 3 THINGS YOU'VE LEARNED TODAY

Which is different in size?

Look at the objects in each box.
Color the object
that is different.

Maze

Help the owl finds its way to the tree!
Color the path

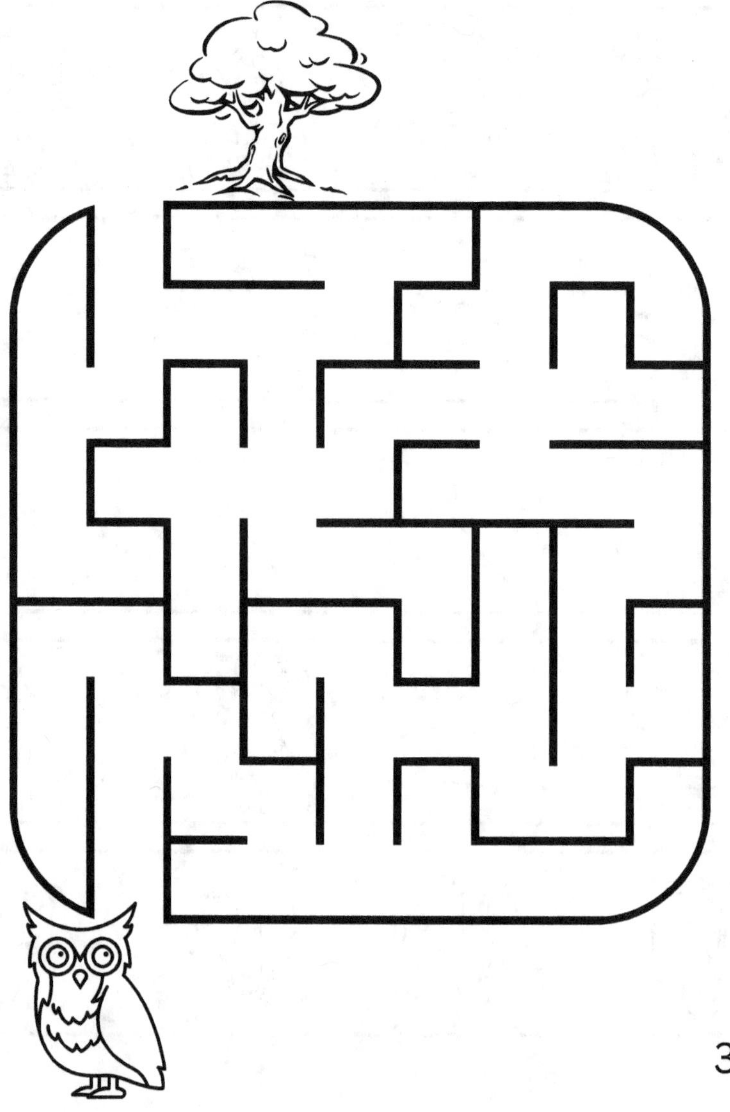

Maze

Help the dragon finds its way to the fire
Color the path

www.ingramcontent.com/pod-product-compliance
Lightning Source LLC
Chambersburg PA
CBHW061319250726
48653CB00002B/967